CELEBRATE HOLIDAYS

Celebrate Diwali

Carol Plum-Ucci

Two girls dance during a Diwali
celebration in Detroit, Michigan.

Enslow Publishers, Inc.
40 Industrial Road
Box 398
Berkeley Heights, NJ 07922
USA

http://www.enslow.com

Library of Congress Cataloging-in-Publication Data

Plum-Ucci, Carol, 1957–
      Celebrate Diwali / Carol Plum-Ucci.
          p. cm. — (Celebrate holidays)
      Includes bibliographical references and index.
      ISBN-13: 978-0-7660-2778-7
      ISBN-10: 0-7660-2778-3
          1. Divali—Juvenile literature. I. Title.
      BL1239.82.D58P64 2007
      294.5'36—dc22

                                                        2006028106

Printed in the United States of America

10 9 8 7 6 5 4 3 2 1

To Our Readers: We have done our best to make sure all Internet Addresses in this book were active and appropriate when we went to press. However, the author and the publisher have no control over and assume no liability for the material available on those Internet sites or on other Web sites they may link to. Any comments or suggestions can be sent by e-mail to comments@ enslow.com or to the address on the back cover.

Every effort has been made to locate all copyright holders of material used in this book. If any errors or omissions have occurred, corrections will be made in future editions of this book.

Illustration Credits: AFP/Getty Images, p. 41; © 1999 Artville, LLC., p. 59; Associated Press, pp. 1, 16, 20, 24, 26, 38, 43, 48, 56, 63, 70, 78, 80, 82, 85, 88, 97, 100, 104; The British Museum/HIP/The Image Works, p. 11; Corel Corporation, p. 92; Dinodia Photo Library, p. 30; Dinodia/ The Image Works, p. 4; Mary Evans Picture Library/The Image Works, p. 9; © 2007 Jupiterimages Corporation, p. 15, Shutterstock, pp. 5, 17, 39, 53, 57, 66, 72, 73, 89, 109 (all); Courtesy of Ben Tubby, p. 68.

Cover Illustration: Associated Press.

CONTENTS

◆ **Chapter 1. The Story of Rama and Sita** 5

◆ **Chapter 2. History of Diwali** 17

◆ **Chapter 3. The Cultural Significance of Diwali** 39

◆ **Chapter 4. Who Celebrates Diwali and Diwali Influences** 57

◆ **Chapter 5. Holiday Symbols** 73

◆ **Chapter 6. Diwali Celebrations Around the World** 89

Diya Dish 108

Glossary 111

Chapter Notes 115

Further Reading 125

Internet Addresses 126

Index 127

Lakshmi

The Story of Rama and Sita

On a special night in October or November each year, our world becomes just a little bit brighter. Across the globe, Hindu families will light candles—many candles—as part of a worldwide celebration. Why? The people want to light the world with a supernatural brightness that brings hope, understanding, and love. As flames light to signify the start of the holiday Diwali, the reflection can be seen in children's eyes across the world.

Diwali, also known as the Hindu Holiday of Lights, began as a celebration in India before recorded history. Therefore, no one is sure how old the holiday is. What is certain is that many myths collided to give the holiday great meaning. The most famous myth surrounding Diwali's origins has to do with the god Vishnu.

Vishnu is a very important god in the Hindu faith, and in the ancient books called the Puranas, it is implied that he is the most important deity. He is known to appear in many forms. One tale very similar to the biblical story of Noah and the Ark tells of Vishnu appearing as a prophetic fish warning about a great flood.[1] In another, he appears as a tortoise, telling the gods to stir up the ocean to get the nectar of immortality. Not only is the nectar churned up, immortalizing the gods, but so is Lakshmi, a beautiful goddess. Vishnu is extremely taken by her and makes her his wife.

Vishnu and Lakshmi have both been known to take on human forms. In the myth most closely associated with Diwali, Vishnu takes the form of the hero Prince Rama. In the tale with Prince Rama, Lakshmi takes the form of his wife, Sita.

The tale is found in an ancient book called the Ramayana. The Ramayana is written like an epic

About the Goddess Lakshmi

The goddess Lakshmi is considered the source of prosperity, success, love, and beauty.

The origin of the word *Lakshmi* is thought to be with several Sanskrit terms. (Sanskrit is the classical language of Hinduism and India).

She is known by other names in certain regions. Those names include Haripriya, meaning "Hari's beloved," Padma, meaning "lotus dweller," and Lokamata, meaning "mother to all in the world."[2]

poem and deals largely with the life of Rama. Here is the famed tale surrounding the holiday of Diwali:

Rama and Sita lived in the royal capital Ayodhya, and from their wedding forward, the city was blessed with great prosperity. Rama's aging father, King Dasaratha, wished to make Rama the next king, as he was the oldest son. The people loved Rama and threw great celebrations throughout Ayodhya in anticipation of his crowning.

However, one of the king's wives was not so happy. Kaikeyi, mother of Bharata, wanted her son to be next in line for the throne. She tricked the king by first getting him to promise that he would fulfill any wish she requested of him. As king, he could not go back on his word. Kaikeyi asked that her son be made the next king and that Rama be sent to live like a hermit for fourteen years out in the woods.

The king was stricken with grief at the request. However, being bound by his oaths, he sent word of the tragedy to Rama and Sita. Rama did not want Sita to come into the woods, but she refused to let him live out his years there without her. They took Lakshman, Rama's favorite brother, to help protect them. The three had many adventures in the forest. Rama and Lakshman fought beasts and evil spirits and always came out the victors.

One day Rama and Sita were sitting under a tree near their cottage, and a giantess named Surpanaka passed by. She fell madly in love with Rama. When she tried to seduce him away from Sita, he simply laughed and said that he was married, and she should try her ardent pleas on his brother. Lakshman also was uninterested and sent her back to Rama. Surpanaka's heart burned with envy toward Sita, and she tried to kill her, thinking that if she were dead, Rama would love her instead. However, Lakshman came to the rescue and cut off the giantess's nose and ears.

The giantess Surpanaka (left) tries to seduce Rama (center), the seventh incarnation of Vishnu, to abandon his wife Sita (right), but he rejects Surpanaka.

Surpanaka persuaded her brother, the demon king Ravana, to kidnap Sita. Ravana was a menacing creature with ten heads. He thought up a plan to kidnap Sita, which was successful. He brought her to his castle on the island of Lanka and kept her prisoner there. He had fallen in love with Sita, and he tried everything to turn her heart from Rama to him. He finally threatened Sita with force, using these words from the Ramayana:

> My cooks shall mince thy limbs with steel,
> And serve thee for my morning meal.[3]
> But Sita remained faithful to Rama.

Rama and Lakshman looked everywhere for Sita. Frequently, they had to fight demons and evil spirits. The monkey king Hanuman became a loyal friend, and with giant leaps, he located Sita on the island. Hanuman employed a local tribe of servants who helped build a bridge to the island in five days.

Opposite: This painting from Tamil Nadu, India, depicts Rama and his friend, the monkey king Hanuman, battling Ravana, Surpanaka's ten-headed brother. The heroes succeed in defeating Ravana and rescue Rama's wife Sita from the island of Lanka.

Hanuman also amassed an army of monkeys, and with Rama and Lakshman, they cross over to Lanka.

Rama fought hard with the army against Ravana's forces and was badly wounded, but he finally met Ravana face to face.

Rama attacked the giant with arrows, but Ravana would not be killed by traditional war weapons. Hence, Rama shot off a fire arrow, whose flame was kindled with a prayer to the gods.[4] It pierced Ravana's heart, and the demon fell dead at his feet.

Throughout his life, Rama had often suspected a secret about himself—that he was the great god Vishnu incarnate.[5] *Incarnate* means "god in the form of a man or animal." After his victory, he learned he was in fact the great god Vishnu incarnate. He also discovered that his wife, Sita, was really Vishnu's wife, the goddess Lakshmi, incarnate. Rama's purpose in life had been to slay the demon Ravana.

Rama, Sita, and Lakshman returned to Ayodhya in a magic chariot. The citizens were overjoyed when they arrived. Light had triumphed over darkness, and everyone shared the wonderful feeling that they were about to enter a period of prosperity and peace unmatched in history.[6]

The people's victory song is found in the Ramayana. In English, its words are these:

Ten thousand years Ayodha,[7] blest
With Rama's rule, had peace and rest.
No widow mourned her murdered mate,
No house was ever desolate.
The happy land no murrain knew,
The flocks and herds increased and grew,
The earth her kindly fruits supplied,
No harvest failed, no children died.
Unknown were want, disease, and crime,
So calm, so happy was the time.[8]

The people of Ayodhya lit candles and oil lamps to symbolize the triumph of good over evil. The happiness over the king's return is still remembered by Hindu people around the world. They light lamps and celebrate prosperity and hope for the future each year. This is the holiday Diwali.

The Incarnations of Vishnu [9]

Rama is only one of the incarnations of Vishnu. He is known as an avatar, someone who descends into the world to restore balance between good and evil. The ten avatars of Vishnu have influenced Hindu culture for thousands of years. He appeared as the following:

1. Matsya the Fish, who saved not only all the creatures but the sacred books from a universal flood.
2. Kurma the Tortoise, who helped make the gods immortal.
3. Varaha the Boar, who brought the earth out of the bottom of the universe.
4. Narasimha the Man-Lion, who destroyed a great demon, Hiranyakasipu and saved his son Prahlad.
5. Vamana, a dwarf who outsmarted the powerful King Bali.
6. Parasurama, who brought peace after many warring kings had created heartache and chaos.
7. Rama, the hero celebrated at Diwali.
8. Krishna, teacher of the famous holy scripture the Bhagavad Gita.
9. Buddha, who taught compassion and peace.
10. Kalki, who will return at the end of the world to punish demons and start a new cycle in time.

L'Inde francaise, 1828. Vishnu, one of the Hindu gods in his second avatar with the body of a turtle.

History of Diwali

Diwali is often considered the most important festival to people of the Hindu faith. Temples, homes, and businesses burn brightly with lights and candles during the five-day celebration. Fireworks fill the air. People wear colorful new clothes, prepare tasty dishes, and usher in the Hindu New Year with music, gifts, and happy hearts.

To understand Diwali, one must first understand a little about the history of Hinduism, the religion from which Diwali comes. Hindu practices and philosophy are older than recorded history. Many rituals and traditions were passed down orally for centuries before they were ever recorded. Therefore, not much is known about the religion's earliest roots. In South Asia thousands of years ago, many people were nomadic, meaning they traveled from place to place. They would exchange their religious ideas and blend with new cultures, teaching the stories and practices that had been taught to them. The area in and around what is now India was very rich in religious diversity.

The original name of Hinduism was "Sanathana Dharma," meaning "righteousness forever" or "that which has no beginning or end."[1] According to most scholars, the term *Hindu* was created by invaders in the sixth century B.C.E.[2] who could not pronounce the name of the Sindhu River properly. Hence, the word's first use was to define a location more than a religion or culture.[3] Some-time before the sixth century B.C.E., the Vedas began to form. The Vedas are a large collection of songs and rituals that were passed down orally for hundreds of years.

Some say as long as three thousand years ago, the Vedas were written down to preserve the writings for descendants. They were written in

Sanskrit, an ancient language of Hinduism, and separated into four sacred books. They included the Rig Veda, Sama Veda, Atharva Veda, and Yajur Veda. Over time the Vedas expanded to include other works, and the vast body of spiritual teaching became known as the Vedic Literatures. These include the Upanishads and the Puranas. The Upanishads contain Hindu philosophy, and the Puranas contain great historical epics or stories.[4]

Two Puranas became a focal point of Hindu life and worship. They are the Ramayana and the Mahabharata. The Ramayana contains the story of King Rama, including his successful return to Ayodhya with Sita that is celebrated at Diwali. The Mahabharata is sometimes thought of as an encyclopedia of Hindu deities, tales, rituals, and beliefs, even though it is an epic poem. It is the longest epic poem in the world, containing over one hundred thousand verses.

The Mahabharata was recorded over a period of several hundred years, ending sometime before 500 B.C.E. The Ramayana may have originally been written down in the first century C.E.[5] As groups of religious people began to accept the Vedas as their primary sacred books, the religion of Hinduism began to solidify.

In 2006, in Varanasi, India, four young boys dressed as Rama and his three brothers during the festival of Bharat Milap in commemoration of Rama's return to Ayodhya after fourteen years in exile.

When the Muslim people invaded South Asia during medieval times, they began calling the Sindhu River the Hindu River. Hence, between the seventh and twelfth centuries, the word *Hindu* described the people living in the provinces of northeast India by the Sindhu River. They called that region *Hindustan*. The term was used once again to describe a location and not a specific religion. The word *Hinduism*, when used by foreigners, did not capture the specifics of the religion. Instead it encompassed a diversity of beliefs and practices.

Today, some people of India do not like the use of the word *Hindu* to describe their faith. For one, it was a word thought up by foreigners. For another, it does not reflect their true culture, devoted spiritual path, and respect for human-kind.[6] Some prefer the words *Sanatan Dharma* to *Hinduism. Sanatan* means "eternal, timeless." Hindu people believe that values and teachings do not become outdated with every new generation or even with a new millennium. All truth applies to all times.[7] Other people do not like Hinduism referred to as a religion. They describe it as "a way of life,"[8] and one feature of Hinduism is that how people behave is more important than what they believe.[9]

Hindu people believe in certain concepts such as dharma. *Dharma* means "law, duty, justice, and virtuousness." Hindu people believe that everyone should try to seek dharma throughout his or her life. They also believe that every soul wants to enjoy our world in a unique way. To fulfill this, the soul enters a cycle of death and rebirth called samsara. The soul leaves the body at death and enters into another body for a new birth. This is the process of reincarnation.

Another such concept is moksha, meaning "salvation." A Hindu belief is that moksha can bring people into nirvana, which is the perfect state, or heaven.

One thing that sets Hinduism apart from other religions is the belief that God is everywhere. In many faiths, things are looked upon as either heavenly or earthly. For example, Jewish, Islamic, and Christian beliefs hold that God is heavenly and man is earthly. But Hindu people believe that God can be in a person, a tree, an animal, or the sky.

They also believe that certain books should be viewed as sacred. The Vedas most closely resemble the Christian and Jewish Bible and the Islamic *Qur'an* in their religious significance. The Brahamanas describe rules for rituals and explanations for why the rituals are important. Rituals from the

Brahamanas and skits from the Ramayana are often performed in Hindu temples.

Finally, the Hindu people believe that celebration is natural and needed in order for men to be happy. India is now considered the home of Hinduism, and it is often spoken of as the Land of Festivals. The Hindu people greatly enjoy celebrations, and, thus, Diwali is a most spectacular and festive time throughout the land.

The Hindu faith has shown remarkable flexibility and has been able to adapt wherever it has gone. The welcoming, friendly atmosphere of today's temples reflect its earliest roots. It reflects the times when nomads first traveled through South Asia, learning new ideas while preserving their own sacred rites.

The Meaning of Diwali

Diwali has evolved into a dazzling worldwide celebration that reflects both timelessness *and* change. The term *Diwali* comes from the Sanskrit word *Deepavali*, meaning "an array of lights." Diwali symbolizes the victory of light over darkness and good over evil. The people of northern India shortened the term to *Diwali*, and the holiday is known by this term today. The Hindu faith has

In 2005, in Allahabad, India, people lit sparklers to celebrate Diwali, the festival of lights, which symbolizes the triumph of good over evil.

embraced new cultures and ideas with which it has come in contact, and thus the holiday is celebrated differently in different parts of the world. Even in different regions of India, the holiday will vary, showing its cultural influences with regional flair. Because of this, it is very hard to give specific descriptions of a "general" Diwali celebration.

In many parts of the world, Diwali is celebrated over five days, while in other places the celebration is only one day. The holiday brings in the Hindu New Year, which falls in the month of October or November, but the actual date of Diwali changes from year to year. That is because the holiday always takes place on the first new moon of the Hindu lunar calendar. Diwali fell on November 1 in 2005 and on October 21 in 2006.

Myths Surrounding the Five Diwali Days

Timeless myths of Hinduism have been continuously passed on, but the evolution of the holiday has barely been recorded. Some of Diwali's most popular myths became part of the holiday before recorded history, and they are still a part of it. These include the myths that make up the five days of Diwali.

The First Day: Dhantrayodashi

In Sanskrit, *dhan* means "wealth," and *trayodashi* means "thirteenth day." Dhantrayodashi always falls on the thirteenth day of the waning moon in the month of Ashwin.[10] One legend features King Hima, a mythological character who had a

In 2006, in Gauhati, India, children lit approximately five thousand earthen lamps during Diwali in hope for world peace.

sixteen–year–old son. The prince was just married, and an astrologist predicted that he would die on the fourth day of his marriage by a snake bite. To protect him on that day, his bride laid all their ornaments and coins in a huge mountain just outside his bed chamber. She lit so many lamps and candles in the house that a blinding light surrounded the prince. She began to tell stories and sing songs so that the prince would not go to sleep.

Yama, the god of death, had disguised himself as a serpent to come to take the prince. But when Yama tried to enter the chamber, he was blinded by the light. He found a comfortable seat on top of the mountain of ornaments and coins and listened to the singing until dawn. At sunrise he slithered quietly away. The young bride had saved her husband from death.[11]

This is how Dhantrayodashi became associated with the lighting of the first lights of the Diwali holiday. The lights show reverence to Yama, the god of death, and they are kept lit throughout the night.

The Second Day: Choti Diwali

The second day of Diwali is often known as Choti Diwali, or "Little Diwali." Choti Diwali is celebrated on the fourteenth day, after Dhantrayodashi. The most popular legend of this day concerns the demon king Narakasur, who had stolen some precious earrings from the Mother Goddess Aditi. He also had kidnapped sixteen thousand daughters of the gods and locked them in his harem.[12]

One of the Mother Goddess's relatives, Satyabhama, was the wife of Lord Krishna and very important in the kingdom. Satyabhama became outraged when she heard of Narakasur's disrespect for the women, and she appealed to Lord Krishna. She asked him for permission to fight and destroy Narakasur. Lord Krishna not only granted her request, but he drove her chariot into battle. Satyabhama cut off Narakasur's head and then released all the harem captives.

Lord Krishna smeared the dead man's blood on his forehead and agreed to marry all the women. When Lord Krishna returned home, the women of his kingdom massaged his war-mangled body with oil and washed him clean.

From this story comes the custom of Hindu people washing early on the day of Choti Diwali before putting on new clothes. Bhudevi, mother of the slain Narakasur, surprised the kingdom by declaring that people should consider the day of her son's death a day of celebration. She also is said to be responsible for much of the merry-making of Diwali.[13]

The Third Day: Chopada Puja

Chopada Puja is considered to be the most important day of Diwali, the third day. It starts the Hindu New Year and is devoted almost entirely to the worship of Lakshmi. Lakshmi is the goddess of wealth and good fortune. She comes down to earth with the gift of prosperity on the night of Chopada Puja.

Many legends exist about Lakshmi, but the Diwali myth concerns her coming to earth as Sita, wife of Rama, as described in chapter one. When Sita and Rama returned from their fourteen years of exile, the people celebrated by lighting lamps all over the city. To this day, people light lamps on this night, believing that the goddess travels the earth and blesses homes that are spotlessly clean and well lit.

Chopada Puja always falls on the new moon. Legend speaks that on this night, the sky will be darker than any other of the year. Lakshmi's own light is said to penetrate the world's darkness with innumerable rays as she visits the earth. The glow

of universal motherhood envelopes the whole world. Lakshmi passes through fields and byways and showers her blessings of prosperity.

When the ceremonies end at sunset on New Year's Day, many sweets and tasty vegetarian dishes are offered to the goddess.

The Fourth Day: Padwa

The fourth day of Diwali, often called Padwa, celebrates the courage of several main mythological characters. Rama quickly became king of Ayodhya after his fourteen years of exile, and people still celebrate the great success in business and industry experienced after his return.

Another Padwa myth honors King Bali, who began to rule a territory called Bhulok. Thus, it is also known as Bali Padyami.[14]

The people of northern India have named this day after one of its sacred rituals called

Opposite: During Chopada Puja, the third and most important day of Diwali, people light lamps in honor of Lakshmi, the goddess of wealth and good fortune, in the hopes that she will bless their home. The figure to the right of Lakshmi is Ganesh, lord of all existing beings.

The Twelve-Month Hindu Calendar[15]

The Hindu calendar follows a cycle of twelve months, but they are different than the months of Western civilization used by most Europeans and Americans. The twelve months of the Hindu calendar follow the cycles of the moon. A cycle runs 29½ days from the beginning of each new moon, so a year lasts only about 354 days. To make up the difference, every two or three years an extra lunar month is inserted. This month is called Adhik and traditionally has been added after the months of Asadha or Sravana.

Here is a list of the Hindu months:

1. **Kartik**	5. **Phalgun**	9. **Asadha**	10. **Sravana**
2. **Agrahayana**	6. **Chaitra**	**Adhik**	11. **Bhadra**
3. **Paus**	7. **Vaisakha**	(once every few years)	12. **Ashwin**
4. **Magh**	8. **Jaistha**		

Each lunar month is divided into two halves of fifteen days each. The new moon begins the first two-week period, called *suklapaksa*, and it is considered the bright half of the lunar month. The full moon begins the second half of the month, known as *krsnapaksa*, or the dark half of the month.

Diwali brings in the New Year, with the new moon of Kartik, which aligns with the Western calendar in the months of either October or November.

Govardhan Puja. According to legend, the people of earth used to worship Lord Indra after monsoon season ended every year. A monsoon is a huge storm that occurs in the Indian and Pacific Oceans, and the wind, rains, and flooding have often wiped out entire villages. The people always thanked Lord Indra for keeping their villages safe.

Like Rama, Krishna is another incarnation of Vishnu, the Hindu god of preservation, who is superior to other deities.[16] One year when Krishna was young, he stopped the people from praying to the god. Lord Indra responded with great fury, and he sent a huge storm to the area near Gokul.

The people became afraid that the storm was coming because they had taken Krishna's advice to stop praying to Indra. Krishna insisted that they should not worship Lord Indra, saying that no one would be harmed. Using only his finger, he picked up Mount Govardhan and protected all the people from the wind and rain. Lord Indra accepted the superiority of Lord Krishna ever after.[17]

The Fifth Day: Bhai Duj

A myth celebrated on the fifth day of Diwali, Bhai Duj, concerns Lord Krishna. After Krishna killed Narakasur, he went to the home of his sister Subhadra. She showed her joy at his arrival by placing a tilak on his forehead and lighting lamps around him. A tilak is a red dot placed on the forehead. Today, many people of the Hindu faith adorn their foreheads with this mark, and this tale of Subhadra is one of its sources.

Another myth features Bhagawaan Mahavir having found nirvana. Nirvana, according to the Hindu faith, is one's final death after many lives and opportunities to become wise. Bhagawaan's brother missed him and was comforted by their sister. Thus, this fifth day of Diwali celebrates the relationships between sisters and brothers.[18]

A final myth reflects the love of siblings that is celebrated at Diwali. Yamraj, a god of death, visited his sister Yami on the fifth day of Diwali. She put a garland around his neck and a tilak on his forehead, and she made him a feast of sweets. They chatted together for hours, very contented. Before leaving, Yamraj gave Yami a special gift, and Yami gave her brother something she had made herself. Yamraj decreed that any man who receives a tilak from his sister will be blessed.[19]

Other Myths Remembered at Diwali

While these are the best-known stories of Hindu mythology, others have arisen, often from stories in the Vedic Literatures, adding to Diwali's flair.

Diwali and Dussehra

The Hindu holiday Diwali is closely associated with another holiday, Dussehra, which falls exactly twenty days before Diwali. In the legend told in chapter one of Rama defeating the great demon Ravana, the day of the actual defeat is celebrated on Dussehra. It leads into the Diwali celebrations of Rama and Sita's homecoming to Ayodhya.

Most Dussehra celebrations include enactments of the Ramayana stories of Ravana's defeat. People sing songs praising Rama and set effigies of Ravana on fire to signify the victory of good over evil. Today, the holiday is seen as an opportunity to reflect on ways to destroy the demon of our ego, and to radiate peace and compassion wherever we go.

Many Hindu people participate in traditions having to do with protecting their families from evil gods of the underworld. In one story from the Puranas, King Bali had become quite powerful and a threat to the gods. He was known as a frightening force but also a very generous king. To end the threat, Lord Vishnu disguised himself as a dwarf. He begged the king for only enough ground that he could cover with three steps, and King Bali agreed.

With that, Vishnu revealed himself in his true and mighty form. His first step covered all of the heavens, and his second step covered the earth. He asked the king where his third step should land, and the king lowered his head, indicating that Vishnu should step on it. With one step, Vishnu pushed him down into the underworld. However, Lord Vishnu remembered King Bali's charity, and he allowed the king to return to earth once a year with a golden lamp of knowledge. The king is now said to light millions of lamps that help rid the world of darkness and ignorance and bring wisdom and love.[20]

One final interesting Diwali tale involves a young boy, Nachiketa. He believed that Yama, the god of death, was black as night and frightening. When he met Yama during the Diwali holidays, he was surprised that the god was calm and dignified. Yama explained that only by passing through the darkness of death can man see the light of higher wisdom, and only through death is his soul free to come together with the Supreme God. After the visitation of Yama ended, Nachiketa felt soothed. He joined in all the celebrations with a free heart.[21]

How long these stories have been told is unknown, but one thing is certain: across the globe during Diwali, they are continuously being retold and reenacted with enthusiasm. Children act them out in skits in the temple. They draw the characters in bright colors on the sidewalks. Families perform various rituals in their homes that bring honor to ancient lore. Temples draw crowds to hear the chants and songs that keep the characters close to millions of hearts.

In 2003, in Bethlehem, Pennsylvania, twelve-year-old Isha Jain performed a dance at the Hindu Temple Society.

The Cultural Significance of Diwali

The Diwali holidays come alive with color. Devotees often put on their most festive outfits and jewelry. Temples and houses glimmer in the tiny lights of thousands of earthen lamps. People dance, sing, worship, and exchange gifts. Celebrations are rich in diversity while holding to traditions older than recorded history.

For all this to occur, preparations are made on a grand scale. Most people agree that getting ready for Diwali can be as exciting as the celebration itself.

Before the holiday starts, people will often thoroughly clean their homes, whether this means scrubbing a small hut on hands and knees or vacuuming posh rugs. It is believed that the goddess Lakshmi loves cleanliness, and she is said to visit a house that is spotless.

Many tasty dishes are prepared, both sweet and salty, and Indian markets throughout the world sell an array of prepared foods.

Diwali Decorations

Children take part in the preparations, often using a powdered substance called rangoli. Rangoli is neutral-colored, but it is mixed with brightly colored substances. Ocher, an iron ore used for coloring, mixes with rangoli to make red and yellow. Turmeric, an ancient Indian herb, also makes yellowish colors when added to rangoli. Vermilion, a red pigment that comes from mercuric sulfide, creates brilliant red colors with rangoli.[1] Children will use the rangoli to make pictures on the sidewalks, creating geometric patterns or images of Lakshmi that might attract and flatter her. Sometimes they paint footprints leading to their houses, which are supposed to represent the

In 2006, in Karachi, Pakistan, a Hindu family prepared for Diwali by drawing geometric patterns on the ground using rangoli, and lighting diyas.

feet of Lakshmi as she comes to earth with her blessings of prosperity. The drawings are similar to sidewalk chalk drawings.

Lights are often considered the most important decoration. They may be electric strings of lights, ancient clay lamps, or various types of candles.

The ancient clay lamps are called diyas. They are simple clay cups, but they can be adorned with jewels or painted bright colors. Diyas can be extremely elaborate, or simple enough that children can follow easy instructions to make them. Some children enjoy making lanterns from bamboo slats and colored paper.[2]

"While I am preparing food, my husband gets the many diyas out of the attic and makes sure they are clean and in order," said one devotee of the Hindu Temple of South Jersey. "He cleans and fills them on the dining room table while I work in the kitchen."

The diyas are filled with oil. Special pieces of cotton resembling cotton swabs with long tails are floated on the oil and lit. The peaceful flame will give a room a soft glow, like that of a candle. Especially in India, many of these lamps are lit on the first night of Diwali. Some Hindu people believe the lights ward off evil spirits. Some believe that the goddess Lakshmi does not like darkness,

During a 2000 Diwali celebration in Manassas Park, Virginia, this teen lit candles. The light has several meanings. Some people believe the light protects them from evil spirits, while others believe Lakshmi will bless the most brightly lit homes.

and on her travels across the world on Diwali night, she will bless the homes that are most brightly lit. In some cities in India, houses, streets, temples, and businesses will be filled with hundreds of the little lights.

In some countries, including the United States, so many little flames are considered a fire hazard. Hindu people in these places will light only a few diyas and will string electric lights in front of their homes.

All Hindu people decorate a small altar in their home, called a puja ghar, in addition to worshiping at the altar of their temples. Various Hindu rituals can therefore be performed right at home.

Favorite Rituals

For most, the celebration of Diwali begins in the evening of the first day. This is when some families light their first lamps. Many people place an oil lamp right outside their door, facing south, to honor Yama, the god of death. It is said that for the rest of the year, a flame should never point in that direction.[3]

An American devotee formerly from Gujarat in western India says, "This first day is the day of devils for us in Gujarat. We put kajal on our eyes. Kajal means 'blaze,' but the substance is a type of black eyeliner. We do it to scare away evil lies. It is fun, like being part of a play, only the whole city is the stage."[4]

Choti Diwali, the second day of celebration, usually starts before sunrise. This is when many Hindu people take ritual baths as a form of preparation for the visit of the goddess Lakshmi. In certain regions, people will apply oil to their foreheads and to the foreheads of their children before bathing.[5]

While bathing, children are sometimes delighted by the sounds of firecrackers in the streets. The fireworks are part of Diwali in many countries where they are legal. In many places in the United States, only professionals are allowed to set off fireworks. People will still light sparklers at the start of the holiday, and in some areas temple officials will arrange for a professional fireworks display. In Britain, small fireworks known as crackers and bangers are allowed, too.

After bathing, family members often worship at their home altars. Sometimes they will sing prabhatiyas, which are holy or uplifting songs generally sung only in the morning. Often, the father will offer a puja to the deities that the family has chosen to place on the home altar. *Puja* means "worship," and Hindus offer many pujas to specific deities on different holidays. During Diwali, a special puja might be offered to the god Vishnu, for his defeat of the demon Narakasur. Other Diwali pujas may be offered to the goddess Lakshmi.[6]

Clothing

The second day of Diwali is often the day when the parties begin. Nearly everyone buys new clothes for the celebrations and worship that follow the ritual bathing. Women will wear the brightest colors imaginable throughout the holidays—brilliant reds, sunny yellows, sky blues, vibrant greens, and sparkly golds. They will wear their best jewels, often Diwali gifts from husbands, brothers, or parents. Festive clothing symbolizes happiness and triumph over darkness.

The traditional dress of Indian women is called a sari, and it can be seen in artwork dating back to 100 B.C.E. A sari is simply a long length of cloth that measures approximately forty-five inches wide and five to nine feet long. Saris can have ornamental borders and a complementing end piece, called the pallu or anchal. A sari is often worn over a choli, or light blouse, that matches the colors in the sari. Women usually wrap the cloth around their waist and then drape an end over one

Celebrating Puja

Puja is important during holiday festivals, but it is also a central element of Hindu worship on a regular basis.

In a Hindu temple, the icons or statues of deities are usually bathed at the start of the puja. The temple priests will rub substances such as sesame seed oil and curd on the deity's "body." The deity will then be dressed in new garments and adorned with jewels and perfume. A red dot of turmeric will be placed on the deity's forehead or the bridge of its nose. The deities will then be offered a meal of boiled rice or sweets while the priests ring bells. The rice will later be eaten by the temple officials or priests.

After the deity's meal, a curtain is drawn back, and devotees can view the displaying of lamps. The priests will wave camphor lamps in a circular motion in front of the deity. Sometimes this is accompanied by drumming, piping, or the blowing of a conch shell.

The circling lamp is known as an aarti lamp. One priest takes the light around, and people cup their hands over the flame and touch their eyes and foreheads. The priests then mark people's foreheads with white ash or turmeric and the puja ends.[7]

In 2005, in Indianapolis, Indiana, this woman offered puja to the gods. She performed a ritual called *aarti*, which involves lighting candles and singing sacred songs to the gods.

shoulder. The methods for wrapping and the appearances come from numerous historical sources.

Most of today's saris belong to the nivi family. The nivi-style drape wraps around the body, starting at the bottom and leaving a series of pleats in the front.[8] Nivi saris are worn all over India as well as in Bangladesh, Pakistan, and Sri Lanka and many communities overseas. The kaccha sari is a similar variation, with the pleats passed between the legs and tucked at the back.[9] The nivi and kaccha styles make walking easy and create a graceful effect that some poets have compared to flower petals in the breeze. The nivi sari was traditionally held in place by tucks in the waistband, but women today generally buy saris with pre-sewn tucks.

Several types of head coverings are popular with women's clothing. The dupatta is a narrow scarf that can be worn over the head or draped over the shoulder. Women from Rajasthan and Gujarat wear bright-colored veils called ordhani.

Men add to the festive flair of Diwali with their own special garments. The dhoti is a rectangular piece of cloth that is tied around the waist in the middle of its length. Each side is wrapped around each leg separately. The brahmin sari is a variation of the dhoti. The cloth is passed between the legs before being wrapped around the body. Generally, the dhoti is a plain color like white or cream, but it will have stripes or simple designs of vibrant color. Different regions have contributed dozens of ways to drape the piece.

Traditionally, a dhoti was often worn with a kurta on top. A kurta is a shirt that comes down to the knees, sometimes slightly above or below. Today, many men wear a pajama with a kurta. Men of southern India will add an angavastram, which is a length of cloth that lays across one shoulder.

Food and Temple

Favorite Diwali dishes are often served throughout the day and evening beginning on the second day, and for the rest of the holidays, food adorns many tables. Friends and family will begin to visit one another's houses to enjoy an ongoing dining experience as part of the celebration.

The Hindu faith does not emphasize any day of the week by calling it the Sabbath; the temple is open every day. The second day of Diwali will bring more people to the temple, but the big temple day is the third day of the holiday. It is the Hindu New Year's Day, and for most temples, it is the busiest day of the year. Temples will be resplendent in the glow of diyas, and the images of the deities will be adorned in the finest of jewels and linens.

These images or statues of the Hindu deities are called murtis, and lengthy lines of devotees will form to make prayers before them. It is believed that the temple is a "home" to the consecrated murtis, and the Hindu priests are their servants. In some of the temples in India, the deities are awakened, bathed, adorned, and offered food in the mornings.[10]

"The temple is so filled on New Year's that we don't worship at any murtis for very long," said a member of the Hindu Temple of South Jersey. "In fact, sometimes a man stands beside each murtis to keep the lines from getting too long. He never says, 'move along,' but we get the idea."[11]

Many temples perform a ritual called the annakut. *Anna* means "food," and annakut involves all the foods offered to the gods. An annakut is a type of prasad, a general offering to the gods. A thaal is a dish prepared for the annakut prasad.

Certain people are selected by a temple to prepare the annakut on an ornately decorated table. These include the best dishes devotees can make, and the table will undoubtedly be thoughtfully prepared. When temple devotees arrive, the annakut is often behind a curtain. During a part of the ceremonies called Darshan of the Annakut, the curtain is drawn back. *Darshan* means "to view." Darshan of the Annakut is the time when devotees view the foods laid out for the gods.

The preparing of food for the gods reflects the Hindu spirit of generosity as well as gratefulness for a good harvest. It is an important part of Diwali ceremonies.

"The annakut is important to us despite that God doesn't eat," the Secretary of the Hindu Temple of South Jersey said with a smile. "When the ceremony ends, all the foods are taken home by those who want it."[12]

Often in temple, children perform skits about Rama and Sita, and cultural dancing may be included. Hindu priests or important local dignitaries may give a talk, emphasizing important Hindu principles.

House Parties

After temple services end, friends and relatives will visit one another and exchange gifts. Dishes are often brought home from the annakut and shared. While the foods vary greatly from region to region, a number of base ingredients are traditional. Puri is a wheat flour dough used to make fried pita bread. Chickpeas make a great base for many dishes, as whatever is presented at the altar is vegetarian.

A diya burns for Diwali.

Sakar is a popular dish with the people of Gujarat in West India. It is little cubes of sugar, said to be popular because the bites are small. After family members have visited several houses, they will be quite full, but no one wants to insult a host by not taking any food. They will settle for a little cube of sugar, and the host is happy.

Gifts

Just about any gift can be given on Diwali, but some traditional gifts have survived the centuries. Among these are jewelry and silver coins bearing the images of Lakshmi and Ganesh. Ganesh is a beloved deity with an elephant's head, and the coins are very popular presents. They symbolize the prosperity for which the holiday is celebrated. Some areas of India are known for the giving of money gifts to all young relatives. A family patriarch, such as a grandfather, will give a gift comparable to a twenty-dollar bill or a fifty-dollar bill to every grandchild, niece, and nephew. In exchange, the children will offer him a charon sparch, which is a type of blessing. *Charon* means "feet," and *sparch* means "touch." The recipients will touch the patriarch's ankle as he gives them the gift to show gratitude and respect.[13]

Sweets go hand in hand with Diwali—both the homemade varieties and the brightly wrapped store purchases. Moti choor ladoo is said to be the most famous of all Diwali sweets. These round delicacies are made from a combination of besan (a gram flour), pistachio, and the spices cardamom and saffron. Another famed sweet, jabeli, is made of sugar and gram flour. Hostesses will place sweets on shiny silver trays and garnish the dishes with diyas and sometimes jewels and flower petals.

Flowers, nuts, and dried fruit are popular gifts, too. Diwali is often a time to give expensive gifts to newlyweds, and these can include money, jewels, cars, and even property.

Like Hinduism itself, Diwali has adapted to the societies in which it can be found. Each region of the world will have its own practices to add to those that have become universal. The crackers and bangers exploding in London bear out different significance than the saffron and rice tikas placed on foreheads in Punjab. However, all rituals, gifts, and traditions worldwide in some way help celebrate the victory of light over darkness and good over evil.

In Katmandu, Nepal, a Hindu woman prays to the Sun God during Chhath, which is celebrated a week after Diwali.

Who Celebrates Diwali and Diwali Influences

India is considered the home of Hinduism, and it is rich in cultural diversity. More than three-fourths of India's one billion people[1] are Hindu, and they bring together traditions from cities, farmlands, suburbs, and coasts, and from sacred lore that has been passed down in each area. When these people migrated to new countries, they took their most beloved traditions and adjusted them to the new culture. People all over the world celebrate

Diwali, using the traditions brought to them by different Hindu people. A temple's celebration will often depend on where most of its devotees came from and which traditions they brought with them.

The diversity of Diwali can best be appreciated by seeing how the people from the different parts of India still celebrate it. People in the rural areas and farmlands are very grateful for the harvest. Their worship has spread with this in mind. People near the ports are most grateful for trade—imports and exports. People in the wealthier areas will celebrate differently from people who live simply.

The people of southern India are said to be responsible for the ritual of applying oils to one's forehead on the second day of Diwali. People there awake before dawn and prepare oil mixed with Kumkum, which is the substance that women use to create the red dot on their foreheads.[2] The people will break bitter fruit and apply the juice-and-oil mixture to their foreheads. This celebrates the legend presented in chapter two of Lord Krishna beheading the demon king Narakasur and wiping his forehead with the demon's blood. The oil mixture represents the blood of Narakasur. The people then bathe in oils using a paste made of sandalwood. This represents how

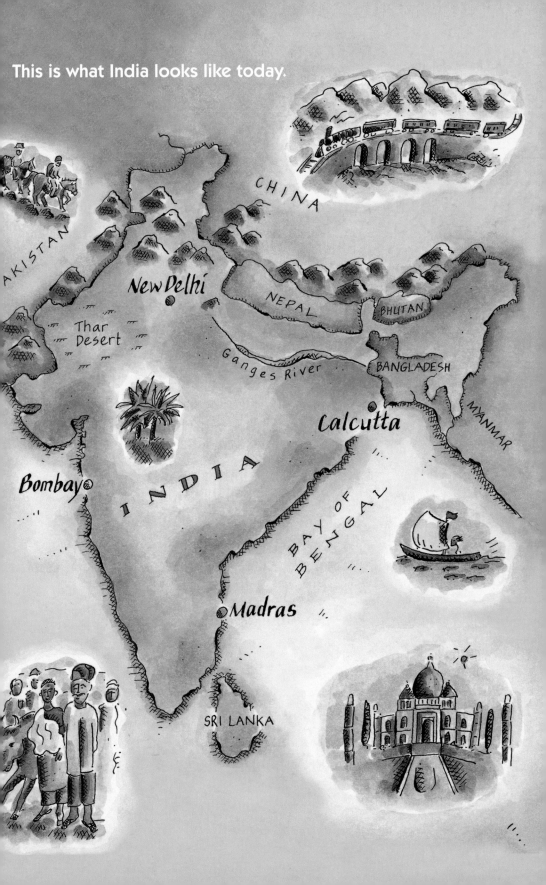

This is what India looks like today.

the women of Lord Krishna's kingdom cleaned him of the soil of battle.[3]

In northern India, people will keep shops open until the afternoon of the third day, believing that good sales will serve as a sign that a successful business year will follow. On nearly every street corner, temporary stages will feature dramatic renditions of the Diwali myths. These shows will continue for several evenings, concluding in the defeat of evil by good.[4]

Gambling is also popular in Northern India. According to legend, the goddess Parvati gambled on this night with her husband, Lord Shiva. She decreed that anyone who gambled on Diwali night would prosper in the coming year. People in northern India play card games with stakes, such as flush and rummy.[5]

Outside the cities, where farms are prominent, Diwali is a time to celebrate the harvest.[6] As the holiday falls in either October or November, it coincides with harvesting, a time that brings hope for the future. The holiday may have actually been started by farmers who wanted to celebrate the end of the harvest season, also known as Kharif.[7] Farm people here are thought to be among the very first to worship of the goddess Lakshmi. Performance of the aarti is one of the oldest rituals of the Kharif or Harvest Festival, involving the lighting of lamps and reciting special chants to the deities. People here also use pauva—semi-cooked rice from the new harvest—to prepare delicacies for celebrations. They offer songs and praises to the gods for providing the fruits of their labors.

People of the Indian States

India has twenty-eight states divided into seven union territories.[8] With their individual histories, traditions, and environments, the states celebrate Diwali with special bits of flair.

Bihar—Northeast India

Bihar is the northeast state that borders Nepal and Bangladesh. It is home to more than 82 million people.[9] The vast majority of these people enjoy celebrating the first day of Diwali with a special tradition. They place kitchen utensils on the altars of the temple. This has to do with the myth of Dhanwantari, known as physician to the gods, who came out of the ocean with a pot in his hand. People from Bihar buy new utensils and lay them on the altar, and Dhanwantari is said to bless them for another year of plenty. The people of Bihar fast all day, which means that they do not eat food while the sun is up. They eat sweets and delicacies after sunset.

On the second day of Diwali, a special custom in Bihar is to make footprints from a rice paste and rangoli. They symbolize the footprints of Lakshmi as she enters a house.

Bihar celebrates a second holiday, Chhath, a week after the Diwali holidays end. For one day and night, many people camp on the banks of one beautiful river, the Ganga (or Ganges), and they perform rituals to the sun god.[10]

Delhi—North Central India

Delhi is the union territory where the capital of India is located. The capital is also called Delhi. The people in this territory are known for their love of the preparations for Diwali. They begin to prepare exactly twenty days earlier, on another holiday called Dussehra. Dussehra is known as the exact day that Rama killed the ancient demon Ravana. To the people of Delhi, Dussehra means that they only have twenty days until Diwali!

Here especially, people consider the twenty days between Dussehra and Diwali the Indian holiday shopping period. It is like the holiday shopping season during December for Christian and Jewish people in the United States. They also clean their

In 2005, in Allahabad, India, Hindus celebrated Dussehra twenty days before Diwali, in honor of Rama's slaying of Ravana. They dipped themselves into the holy water of the Sangam, where the three rivers, the Ganges, the Yamuna, and the Saraswati meet.

houses thoroughly, buy new clothes, paint their walls, and decorate streets and businesses.

On the third day of Diwali, the people of Delhi keep their shops open until the afternoon, because they believe that good sales on that day predict good business throughout the year. Many street corners will feature a makeshift stage and a reproduction of the story of Rama and Sita.[11]

Gujarat—West India

In the western state of Gujarat, on the Arabian Sea and the Gulf of Camboy, the people celebrate Diwali for the five full days. It is also an area where people shop weeks in advance for new clothing, sweets, gifts, and fireworks. As in Bihar, children here also draw footprints with rice flour and rangoli on sidewalks and walls to signify the footprints of Lakshmi as she comes to visit their homes.

In Gujarat, shops will stay open until New Year's Day, but all other businesses close on the second day of Diwali. They do not reopen until the fifth day after the New Year, called Labh Pancham. For businesspeople, it is a time for taking vacations, and they will visit with friends and relatives throughout the holiday.[12]

Kashmir—Northeast India

Some of the oldest rituals known to Hinduism find their roots in the northeastern state of Kashmir. This area is actually mentioned in the Nilmat Puran, an old and sacred text about festivals. The region was called the Sukhsuptika in the ancient writings, which literally means "sleep with happiness."

Thus, the people of Kashmir participate with great fervor. Everyone except children and sick people will fast for a whole day and worship Lakshmi after sunset. Earthen lamps are found everywhere during Diwali. All places will glow from the presence of thousands of little lights, including shops, businesses, road crossings, cremation grounds, riverbanks, barns, and courtyards.[13]

Maharashtra—Western India

Hindus in Maharashtra strictly adhere to bathing rituals in early morning. They bathe in a combination of oil and uptan, meaning "paste," which contains gram flour and fragrant flowers. Throughout the time designated for ritual baths, the sounds of fireworks fill the air. The period ends with devotees enjoying a dish of steamed vermicelli, a type of rice, served with milk and sugar, or puffed rice with curds.[14]

People here often begin Diwali festivities with Vasu-baras, a celebration held in honor of cows. Cows are a symbol of motherhood in the Hindu faith, and married women perform a prayer of blessing over cows that are having calves. The tradition symbolizes a woman's gratitude toward the creatures for providing dairy and nutrients for their families.[15]

In some parts of India, cows are considered scared. This cow was dressed up for a festival.

Punjab—North India

The state of Punjab got its name from the words *Panj Aab*, which mean "five rivers." The area is known for its prosperity and days of celebration. It is culturally diverse, and people of other religions join in the Diwali celebrations. In Punjab villages, cows are especially worshiped because they are said to be an incarnation of the goddess Lakshmi. Farmers will sow the seeds for winter crops. The second day of the New Year is known here as Tikka. The tradition on Tikka is for sisters to honor their brothers, and girls place the tilak on their brother's foreheads to ward off evil.

The four-hundred-year-old Golden Temple Amritsar in Punjab has a long, elegant pool in front of its entrance. In 1577, the first stone of the foundation was laid for the temple during Diwali by a group of Hindu worshipers called the Sikhs. During that period, a very important Sikh leader, Guru Hargobind Sahib, and fifty-two kings were imprisoned by the Muslim emperor. All of them were released during Diwali. The people celebrate with great fervor in Punjab, to remember the religious freedom they were granted during the holiday. At night, people float hundreds of different-colored lamps on the water in the pool. It becomes a rainbow of colors, especially when the

The Golden Temple Amritsar in Punjab was built by the Sikhs four hundred years ago. People float many colorful lamps in the grand pool at the front of the building during Diwali.

massive fireworks display lights the sky over the temple.[16]

Orissa—Southeast India

The state of Orissa is known for a special ritual. Families call upon their deceased ancestors in a ceremony that involves lighting plant stems, and the dead relatives are said to come and take the aroma back to heaven. The ritual starts with the family members' drawing an image of a boat out of rangoli. The boat has seven chambers, and various spices are put in each one. The center chamber contains the prasad, or offering to the gods.[17] At the beginning of the worship, everyone in the family lights a bundle of jute stems from the flame in the center chamber. They chant, calling to their ancestors. When the ceremony ends, the family will celebrate with firecrackers and by keeping all lamps lit. Windows and doors are kept open for Lakshmi to pass through at her whim.[18]

West Bengal—East India

West Bengal is actually in east India, just west of the country of Bangladesh. Here, people place a special emphasis on the deity Kali. This makes their celebration a little different than in other parts of India, where most emphasis is on the goddess Lakshmi. Kali is considered a fearful goddess and not one who is usually beloved like Lakshmi.

In West Bengal, a ceremony called Kali Puja is popular. The people here give special parties for gambling, drinking, and feasting. There is little emphasis on new clothes or jewelry. The people give gifts, but they are often limited to sweets and fruits.[19]

Uttar Pradesh—North Central India

Uttar Pradesh is the home of the famous city of Varanasi, also known as Benares, on the northern

In Amritsar, India, Hindu devotees parade in monkey costumes during Dussehra to commemorate Ravana's defeat by Lord Rama and the monkey general Hanuman.

bank of the Ganga, or Ganges River. The city is sacred to people of all branches of Hinduism, as it is considered a reverent place to live out one's final days and meet death. Sacred rituals associated with death are performed there twenty-four hours a day.[20]

On the first full moon following Diwali, people gather at the two great rivers in Varanasi and leave thousands of earthen lamps. Visitors from across the world come to watch the multitude of dots twinkle and glow.

Himachal Pradesh—North India

The state of Himachal Pradesh is nestled at the foot of the Himalayas. The state is rich with ancient traditions as well as rural charm. People here celebrate Diwali by painting over the mud walls of houses with whitewash and cow dung. In some courtyards, they cheerfully paint a red-and-black square decorated with birds and animals, and they make flower garlands to adorn the dwellings. These are supposed to be particularly pleasing to the goddess Lakshmi. This area is also known for celebrating Diwali by lighting clay lamps in memory of departed loved ones, and the people here sacrifice goats.[21]

Holiday Symbols

Entering the temple during the Diwali holidays, people are awed by the shimmering lights of hundreds of little diyas. The diyas are symbols. Voices rise in songs and chants. This music is rich with symbolism. People kneel and offer prayers to a murtis. A murtis is considered God in the form of a statue, or a symbol of one incarnation of God. Everything from the murtis' dress to the objects it holds are highly symbolic.

Hinduism is rich with symbolic tradition, and to fully appreciate Diwali, one must first understand the meanings of some of the most eminent symbols.

Candles, Lamps, and Lights

To people throughout history, light has been a symbol of brightness, understanding, hope, and triumph. Hardly a religion exists that does not use candles as part of worship, and the Hindu people place enormous emphasis on various forms of illumination during the Hindu Holiday of Lights. From the smallest huts to the largest mansions worldwide, it is rare to find a Hindu dwelling not adorned with at least one row of diyas. The soft glow of lights symbolizes the victories in ancient tales.

When Rama and Sita returned to Ayodhya after their fourteen years of exile, the people lit candles to celebrate their victory over Ravana. Thus, the lights symbolize goodness triumphing over evil, or "light" triumphing over "darkness."

In the story celebrated on the first day of Diwali, the newly married son of King Hima needed protection from Yama, the god of death. His bride lit so many earthen lamps throughout their house that Yama was hypnotized and left without harming the prince. In this tale, light symbolizes victory over death.

In the story celebrated on the fourth day of Diwali, Lord Krishna thrust King Bali into the underworld by stepping on his head. The generous yet frightening king was allowed to return to earth once a year with a golden lamp of knowledge. He is now said to light millions of lamps each Diwali holiday. This story shows light as a symbol of both generosity and wisdom.

Most of all, light is a symbol of peace on earth and love of one's fellow man. While all the various tales reflect this, the symbol is used to remind people of the importance of always being kind, generous, wise, and hopeful. One famous Indian poet, Gurudev Rabindranath Tagore, captured the true essence of Diwali when he wrote these words:

> The night is black
> Kindle the lamp of LOVE
> With thy life and devotion.[1]

Ritual Bathing

The ritual baths, also known in some places as holy baths, are a worldwide part of Diwali celebrations. The tradition primarily grew out of the story of Lord Krishna and Sayabhama killing the demon Narakasur. The women of his kingdom washed Lord Krishna clean from the filth of battle, symbolizing victory after a long and difficult period.

Along with using symbols in rituals, people like to imitate the things their heroes did to celebrate Diwali. This is another way of remembering an important tale. Lord Krishna returned home on the second day, and thus, most people take part in ritual baths before sunrise on that day.[2] As the women of his kingdom applied scented oils to his skin, people today still use scented oils and soaps in ritual bathing. These include utanh and sandalwood paste.[3]

The people of southern India introduced a part of the ritual that takes place just before bathing. They symbolize the blood of the slain Narakasur by mixing Kumkum with oil. They apply the red mixture to their foreheads, just as Lord Krishna smeared the demon's blood on his own forehead after killing him. The smearing of blood was Lord Krishna's way of symbolizing victory. The people then break bitter fruit, which symbolizes the broken head of the demon.

The Tilak and Bindi

After bathing, people will put on their bright new clothes and jewelry. Many also wear a dot on their

The Most Well-Known Hindu Deities[4]

Many Hindu villages have their own regional deities, which are thought to look after the daily concerns of the people. The better known and universally worshiped deities are thought to take care of the universe overall. Here is a list of the more widely known Hindu deities:

Annapurna, goddess of cooking and food

Balrama, brother of Krishna and the divinity of strength

Bhuvaneshwari, queen of the phenomenal world

Brahma, the creator of the universe

Buddha, the ninth incarnation of Vishnu

Dhanwantari, physician of the gods

Dhumavati, an ugly and fearful goddess, known as Divine Mother when the earth was under water

Durga, an incarnation of the Devi, or Mother Goddess

Ganesh, lord of all existing beings, having an elephant's head

Ganga, a god incarnated as the Ganga (Ganges) River

Garuda, king of the birds, messenger between gods and men

Hanuman, monkey deity known for courage and selflessness

Indra, king of the gods and ruler of the heavens

Kali, a fearful incarnation of the Divine Mother; goddess of time

Kartikay, scientist of the gods

Krishna, eighth incarnation of Vishnu, god of love and joy

Kurma, second incarnation of Vishnu, a tortoise

Lakshmi, goddess of light, beauty, prosperity, and good fortune

Matangi, a fearful incarnation of the Divine Mother

Maya, goddess of illusions or things veiled

Rama, seventh incarnation of Vishnu and central character of the Ramayana

Saraswati, goddess of knowledge, music, and the creative arts

Shakti, destroyer of demonic forces who restores balance to the universe

Shiva (or Shiv), destroyer of the world, who joins his power with Brahma, the creator, and Vishnu, the preserver

Sita, the incarnation of Lakshmi, who is central as Rama's wife in the Ramayana

Vamana, a dwarf and the fifth incarnation of Vishnu

Vishnu, preserver and protector of creation

In Allahabad, India, a Brahmin, a member of
the Hindu priestly caste, makes a red line on
his forehead to symbolize a third "spiritual"
eye, which opens his soul to God.

forehead. The dots hold different meanings and different names. A tilak is a red dot worn on the forehead after any puja. It is also known as *tika* and *bottu*. In a temple, the priest will make a red line on a man's forehead and a dot on a woman's forehead. For men, the line symbolizes a third or "spiritual" eye, which opens their soul to the goodness of God. It also symbolizes the Supreme Being himself, God, who shows himself through the many gods worshiped in Hinduism.

Another dot to the forehead is called the bindi. Women wear this dot regularly. A red bindi used to be almost exclusively a symbol of marriage, but today unmarried women wear it also. In parts of southern India, girls wear a black bindi when they reach puberty. Most young girls now wear the bindi to match their clothing.[5] It also marks a place on the body that could be considered a third or "spiritual" eye.

Today, women wear bindis with ornate designs. On Diwali, it is assured that Hindu women everywhere will wear the symbol of beauty and spirituality on their forehead.

Symbols Associated with Lakshmi

In most regions of the world, Diwali centers around worship of the goddess Lakshmi. The murtis of

In Allahabad, India, a woman sells figurines of Lakshmi, the goddess of wealth, who offers a blessing of well-being with her lower left hand and a blessing for prosperity with her lower right hand.

Lakshmi is very rich in symbolism. *Lakshmi* comes from a Sanskrit word *laksme* which means "goal." The goddess Lakshmi represents life's goals, both for prosperity and spiritual achievement.

Lakshmi is usually seen standing or sitting on a lotus and she has four hands. Two hands hold lotus flowers. The lower right hand offers blessings for prosperity, and the lower left is in a position to offer a benediction type of blessing, which will follow worshipers until they return to the temple next time. The lotus flower symbolizes the realization of Self as the foremost goal in life.

Her four hands symbolize the four blessings she gives to human beings, which are: dharma (duty), artha (wealth), kama (sensual pleasure), and moksha (the final liberation from tribulation).

Lakshmi always wears a garland of lotus flowers and is often accompanied by two elephants. Sometimes the elephants are adorning her with garlands, and sometimes they pour water over her, representing power and purity.

Lakshmi's complexion varies in different artwork and murtis as well. When her skin is dark, it symbolizes her connection with Lord Vishnu as his wife and constant companion. When her skin is golden, it represents fortune and wealth. When she is white, she symbolizes the highest powers

In Allahabad, India, a young Hindu girl shows her devotion to Lakshmi during Diwali.

of nature, which gave great life force to the universe. When she is pinkish, she reflects compassion and mercy as the mother of all beings.

Sometimes Lakshmi is pictured sitting in a temple of her own instead of accompanying Lord Vishnu. In this instance she usually sits on a lotus throne with four items in her hands: a lotus, a conch shell, a pot of nectar, and a fruit. The nectar pot symbolizes her blessings of immortality. The fruit reflects people's actions in life that proceed from her blessings. The conch symbolizes her origins, as she is said to have been born from a mythical milk ocean.[6]

Symbols in Worship

A special Lakshmi Puja, or worship of Lakshmi, is offered to the goddess on the third day of Diwali. Worship of the goddess Lakshmi is said to bring prosperity and good fortune in business throughout the New Year.

Vaishali Patel, a medical student in the United States, remembers fondly the ritual performed by her family when they were living in Gujarat, West India. They performed the puja in their living room.

"We would wash coins with five ingredients. They are milk, honey, yogurt, ghee (purified butter), and something else sweet like sugar. We would wash the coins clean with water and put them on a shiny copper tray. We would then apply Kumkum, the base used by women to put the dots on their foreheads. We would dip with our ring finger, and place a dot on the god's face showing in the coin. Next, we would sprinkle the tray with a few pieces of rice and flower petals."[7]

Then they would worship the goddess with chants and prayers.

At temple and home, people often lay checkbooks and business ledgers or other forms of financial records on the altar. This part of the Lakshmi Puja symbolizes the belief that the goddess will bring prosperity throughout the coming year.

Parimal Parikh, treasurer of the Hindu Temple of South Jersey, speaks of how Hindu worship has always fit into the times, including its Lakshmi Puja. "This year, we saw many computer CD-ROMs on the altar for the Goddess to bless, and prior to this year, it was the floppy disks. It doesn't matter to her."[8]

Temple services on this third day of Diwali are different in every temple. However, each service is sure to be rich in symbolic rituals and objects. Devotees might sing a kirtan, which is a Hindu devotional song. They might participate in an aarti. In Sanskrit, *Aa* means "towards," and *rati* means "the highest love for God." An aarti is ritual in which people offer light to the gods with candles. *Aarti* can also mean a sacred song, with the music symbolizing the light. People may participate in a

In Bombay, India, children paint their faces and carry
lamps in celebration of Diwali.

Darshan of the Annakut, which is the viewing of the deities, with all the food carefully prepared for them.

These ancient rituals are combined with performances that are often extremely modern, such as slide shows or video messages from important Hindu leaders in India. The blending of the old and new with grace and zeal is a mark of the Hindu faith. It is a symbol in itself of the diplomacy that has allowed the religion to do more than survive. It now reaches into all corners of the world.

Other Hindu Festivals[9]

India is often called the Land of Festivals, and many celebrations of the Hindu faith were born there. Many festivals are indigenous to a specific region, but the holidays most known among devotees worldwide are as follows:

Krishna Janamastami: Falls in the month of Sravana (July–August) and celebrates Krishna's birthday.

Rakhi Bandhan: Falls on the full moon of Sravana (July–August) and celebrates the close relationship between brothers and sisters. Sisters tie colored threads around their brothers' wrists.

Ganesh Caturthi: Falls in the month of Bhadra, (August–September) and commemorates Ganesh, god with the elephant head.

Dussehra: Falls in the month of Ashwin (September–October) and runs for ten days in some places, called *navaratri*, meaning "nine nights." The tenth day celebrates the victory of Rama and his monkey army over the demon Ravana.

Sivaratri: Falls in the month of Magh (January–February) to commemorate the god Shiva.

Holi: Falls in the month of Phalgun (February–March) to commemorate the grain harvest in some places. It is best known for people's boisterous behavior—they throw colored water and powder in the streets.

In early 2006, in Indianapolis, Indiana, a large crowd of eager Hindu devotees await the opening of the new Hindu Temple of Central Indiana.

Diwali Celebrations Around the World

The Hindu culture tends to be very tolerant and welcoming to other faiths. Even in foreign countries, Diwali is becoming more of a community-wide celebration. People of all faiths may participate in the grand festivities. Civic leaders enjoy giving speeches about neighborly conduct and unity at these events.

From America to Guyana to Britain to Australia to Indonesia, one will find the echoes of ancient Diwali traditions mixed with the discoveries of a new homeland.

Malaysia

Malaysia lies eastward from India, across the Bay of Bengal. Known for its diversity of faiths and traditions, Malaysia hosts an 8 percent Hindu population. Diwali is called Hari Diwali there. It is celebrated jointly with a Malaysian festival called Hari Raya, so some people have coined the term *Deeparaya* for both.

Diwali festivities begin with oil baths and include visits to temples and prayer at home altars. Diyas here are filled with coconut oil. People blend Indian and Malaysian art together to make unique decorations that adorn houses, streets, hotels, businesses, and government buildings. Great celebrations take place in the rural areas, and people will find any means of transportation out of the cities to enjoy them. People celebrate in the market places by watching dance performances, getting henna tattoos, and eating Thai, Malaysian, and Indian foods.[1]

Malaysia is one of the few countries to have made Diwali a national holiday. The prime minister will remind people to celebrate diversity and enjoy the faiths of others. While giving one Diwali speech, Prime Minister Datuk Seri Abdullah Ahmad Badawi said, "Let us join hands, multiply our efforts and forge ahead with one objective irrespective of race and religion, to take our beloved country to ever greater heights of glory, distinction and excellence."[2]

Nepal

Nepal, a country that sits at the foothills of the Himalayas, is the only Hindu monarchy in the world. The people here know Diwali as Tihar. In Nepal, the first day of Diwali honors the cow, which is a symbol of motherhood and fertility. The people prepare food and feed the cows, sometimes adorning them with garlands. This shows their appreciation for the food the animals bring throughout the year and for the agricultural work they perform.[3] The second day is devoted to dogs in honor of Bhairava (the terrifying manifestation of Shiva) and his dog Vahana. People prepare special food for their dogs.[4] On the third day, people uphold the Indian tradition of lighting lamps to celebrate New Year's. Day four is dedicated to Yama, the god of death, and people

In Prambanan, Indonesia, hundreds of dancers bring the Ramayana to life onstage. The epic story tells of the adventure of Lord Rama, the Hindu god Vishnu in human form, and his wife Sita, the goddess Lakshmi incarnate.

pray for good health and long life. Day five is like the majority of modern Diwali celebrations—dedicated to brothers and sisters. Sisters pray for their male siblings to have prosperity and health, and they serve a tasty feast.

Mauritius

Mauritius is an island east of Madagascar, which is just east of the continent of Africa in the Indian Ocean. Over 60 percent of the population is of Indian descent, and 80 percent of these Indians practice the Hindu faith. The natives believe that Diwali was celebrated even before King Rama's return after his fourteen years in exile. People celebrate by placing lamps in rows to form images, and they burn firecrackers, known there as "crackers," to scare off evil spirits.

Mauritius is another very diverse place, and it is often said to be a great example of how the main religions of the world can coexist with each other. Leaders from the Christian and Islamic groups there send warm messages to the Hindus during Diwali.

The Catholic Bishop of Port Louis in Mauritius said this in one holiday message: "Religious festivals are a precious gift towards the social interaction of the Mauritian people. . . . May the light that we celebrate at Diwali show us the way and lead us together on the path of peace and social harmony."

Yacoob Dawood, a well-known Muslim leader there, encouraged the people of Mauritius to use Diwali to "embrace understanding, fellow-feelings and mutual respect . . . which no doubt will result in the progress of our plural society."[5]

South Africa

West of Mauritius is the country of South Africa, located at the southern tip of the African continent. South Africa at one time boasted the largest Indian immigrant population in the world. Today, almost one million people of Indian descent make their home there. About 65 percent of the population is Hindu, so Diwali is a noteworthy holiday. Celebrations mirror those going on in India, including lighting clay lamps, burning incense, distributing sweets, and going to the temple.[6]

Most of the Indian population lives near Durban, a city by the sea. For the past several decades, beach celebrations have drawn the biggest crowds ever seen on the Durban shores. Festivities include music, dancing, fireworks, and a huge bazaar. One of the country's leading banks, FSB, decided to sponsor the entire Durban festival

Gift Hampers: A Popular Gift of the Millennium

One of the most popular worldwide gifts during Diwali is the gift hamper. Gift hampers are much like gift baskets, but filled with Diwali treats and fun. They can be purchased already made, but many people like to make up their own.

Since fireworks, lights, and diyas are popular on the holidays, a hamper often includes candles and sparklers. Treats might include cashews, known in many places as kaju, and roasted almonds, known as badam. Dried fruit is also a favorite gift. This would include sukhi khubani (dried apricots), sukhi khajoor (dates), ananas (pineapple), and aam (mango).[7]

recently because it was drawing people from all faiths and backgrounds.

South Africa has seen many wars and tragic times. In 2001, the country's president, Thabo Mbeki, asked people to reflect on their own victories during Diwali.

"The celebration marking the legendary return of (Hindu god) Lord Ram[a] and Sita from exile symbolizes the victory of divine forces over those of wicked oppression, and South Africans can well relate to this experience, having emerged from a period of intense oppression," said the president. "May you continue, together with all other South Africans, to light the lamps leading towards a better life for all in our beloved country."[8]

Great Britain

Hindu people throughout Europe celebrate Diwali, but a sizable Hindu population lives in Great Britain. Great Britain's October–November weather is wet, cool, and windy. Indian people there celebrate Diwali fervently to help ward off longings for the more temperate climate of their homeland. Hindu people will visit the local temple to worship at the shrine of the goddess Lakshmi, and after saying prayers to her, they celebrate with house parties. They will eat sweets and burn incense and candles. The blowing of a conch shell is popular in Britain. The conch symbolizes the life that comes out of the sea, and it is blown before important announcements and different parts of religious ceremonies.[9]

Guyana, South America

Far across the Atlantic is the country of Guyana on the northeast shores of South America. The first

In London, two women partake in the first Hindu holiday to be celebrated in Parliament. Far from their native land, many Hindus bring the warmth and magic of Diwali to their new homes.

known Hindu people there arrived in the middle 1800s, and today the population of Guyana nears 33 percent Hindu. Some of the Diwali rituals hold special meanings in Guyana. People distribute sweets to show the importance of sharing and serving others. Recipes generally include kheer, pera, or barfi. Kheer has a pudding base, and pera and barfi are milk-based fudges.[10] People eat spicy curry dishes out of lotus leaves. The ever-important lights are so emphasized here that some households will light over five hundred diyas.[11] To the people of Guyana, wearing new clothes is especially meaningful in this festival. They believe that wearing new garments symbolizes healthy bodies with healthy souls.[12]

A tradition of more than twenty years has been the Guyana Diwali Motorcade. It is an enormous parade that runs for five hours down the sea coast. Businesses and families decorate their cars with thousands of lights and Diwali themes. Dazzling floats are included, and prizes are awarded in different categories.[13]

Trinidad and Tobago

Trinidad and Tobago, often called the twin islands, are located in the southernmost part of the Caribbean. Only seven miles from the coast of

Venezuela, they have adopted Venezuela's zest for colorful celebration. Indian migrants make up 43 percent of the population. Diwali celebrations are often used to encourage unity among the many diverse inhabitants of the islands. These include Christians, Muslims, Indian Trinidadians, and African Trinidadians. Anything written about the holiday, such as fliers and promotional materials, will bear the official government imprint or seal to show the support of leadership. And ministers and government officials participate in festivities.

Celebrations continue for over a week and mirror India's emphasis on the domination of good over evil. Headquarters for the National Council of Indian Culture sponsor and promote numerous holiday festivities that change from year to year.[14]

Italy, the Holy Catholic See

The Vatican, home of the pope in Rome, has often participated in Diwali. Each year, a high official from the Vatican will publish a letter of tidings to Hindu people around the world. In 2003, Archbishop Michael Fitzgerald sent out a message to people of the Hindu faith worldwide.

He called Diwali "the feast which you celebrate according to your venerable religious tradition," and "a time for families to get together, and

In Port of Spain, Trinidad and Tobago, this girl illuminates the night in celebration of Diwali.

celebrate in a meaningful way the rites prescribed by the ancient dharma."

He wrote that he hoped Diwali would give all men and women an opportunity to renew efforts for worldwide peace. "I have always been impressed by the fact that on the occasion of Diwali there are some Hindus who make every effort to bring about reconciliation within families and between neighbors, friends and acquaintances. Could not Catholics and Hindus extend these efforts to bring about wider reconciliation and a more lasting peace in our towns and villages and indeed throughout our countries and the world at large?"

He continued, ". . . the more we commit ourselves to promote the dignity of every human person, the more our religious traditions will become credible in the eyes of others."[15]

Diwali Celebrations in the United States

A 2004 nationwide population poll showed that over two million people of Hindu faith make their home in the United States.[16]

Vaishali Patel, a visiting student from Gujarat, said, "When I was growing up in India, every family on my street had somebody in America."[17]

One will find a great number of American traditions woven into Hindu festivities, and guests of honor have included some of the most important people in the United States.

Civic leaders have taken the holiday's messages of peace, friendship, and unity to help bring entire cities together. In 2004, the mayor of New York City, Michael Bloomberg, held a Diwali celebration at Gracie Mansion, the historic home of the New York mayor. Among those invited were the Consul General of India, President of the Association of Indians in America, and the Immigrant Affairs Commissioner. The New York City police chief and other important city dignitaries also came to celebrate.[18]

In Washington, D.C., honorable guests of the temple ceremonies have included the Minister for Personal and Community Affairs from the Indian Embassy, plus the State senators and representatives from the Maryland Governor's Office.

In many places, the dignitaries have been interspersed with other people of all faiths. Hindu people enjoy inviting their American friends to help them celebrate. In Westchester, New York, a state-of-the-art temple was completed in 2003. Temple members invited the head electrician and construction workers as well as the mayor.

The Dallas, Texas, Diwali celebration welcomed the entire families of many executives from the Dallas/Fort Worth Metroplex.

Edison, New Jersey, is sometimes affectionately known as Little India, as the population of Indian newcomers has swelled. Former Governor James McGreevey and Governor Jon Corzine have attended Diwali temple festivities in Edison. More celebrations, including the one held in Cherry Hill Township, New Jersey, feature speeches by the mayor or the local council members.[19]

If a temple is new, the celebration of Diwali can be spectacular. In 2004, newly erected temples in Chicago and Houston were inaugurated during Diwali. The skies over both cities were lit with uninterrupted fireworks that lasted half an hour.[20]

People who are not familiar with the Hindu faith will often find the lights, celebration, and greetings from Hindus a memorable experience.

"I went to the local temple just because a Hindu friend asked me," said one American college student from South Jersey. "It was really beautiful. The lights and the decorating must have taken weeks to get so perfect. I came away feeling like I'd been touched."[21]

One photographer in Missouri thought she was going to the ceremony just to take pictures for

In Los Angeles, California, devotees from the Valley Hindu Temple in Northridge pray for peace and offer light to the god during the fourth day of Diwali. They are also celebrating the Hindu New Year 2058.

her newspaper. She later wrote in thanks, "As soon as I walked into your temple I saw your Guru's photo and felt like He was a real person present and looking at me. During my photograph sessions I sensed that He was telling me how to take pictures and it looked like He was posing for me. I saw real divinity."[22]

"Our temple is wonderfully crowded on Diwali Day," said a young attendee of the Hindu Temple of South Jersey. "We know not to pray at any statue for more than a minute or two, or it will create lines and be disrespectful to the guests."[23]

Hinduism has flourished over thousands of years because it has always been a transportable religion. As its first believers were nomads who traveled from one place to another in southern Asia, the most important elements were the oral traditions, and its followers exchanged ideas and artifacts that reflected its adaptability. That adaptability is still flourishing in America.

The Cherry Hill Township, New Jersey, temple, featured a giant milk chocolate Hershey bar as one of the sweets in the annakut feast. The Washington, D. C., celebration presented a magic show for children that blended some Eastern and Western illusions to help teach the meaning of the holiday. The Philadelphia temple, which hosted numerous guests, featured the modern technology of giant overhead screens so that all would be able to see a show on the holiday's history.

The same welcome of technology has allowed devotees in temples across America to receive video blessings from noteworthy leaders, such as the Pramukh Swami Maharaj of India.

Diwali has become a worldwide celebration that incorporates some of India's oldest traditions, sending them to the farthest corners of the world. The Hindu Holiday of Lights provides an opportunity to remember that peace and the "light" of understanding are more important today than ever before. As airplanes and phones and email and television draw people ever closer together, people are learning to respect their neighbors and be accepting of cultures different than their own. People understand that next-door neighbors, while different from them, are worthy of dignity. Diwali provides a time for the whole world to celebrate unity in diversity.

Thousands of years ago, a famous Hindu prayer was softly whispered by the nomads traveling across the Indian subcontinent. Today, on Diwali and throughout the year, it is spoken by thousands of voices across the world:

From the unreal lead us to the real
From darkness lead us to the light
From death lead us to immortality.
Peace. Peace. Peace.[24]
　　　—Brihad Aaranyaka Upanisad 1:2:28

Diya Dish

Diyas are lit throughout the Diwali holiday. You can make a version of a diya and use it to hold items like candy or coins.

You will need:

- ✔ **air-drying clay**
- ✔ **poster paint** (optional)
- ✔ **paintbrush** (optional)
- ✔ **white glue** (optional)
- ✔ **glitter** (optional)

What to Do:

1 Roll air-drying clay into the size of a small lemon.

2 Use your thumbs to gently push in the center of the ball to make a bowl. Use your fingers to smooth out the clay. Make sure the clay is the same thickness all around so it dries evenly. Let dry.

3 If you wish, paint the diya dish. Let dry.

4 Your diya dish is ready to hold wrapped candy, coins, or whatever you choose!

Use any color clay you wish.

Paint your diya with poster paint.

Experiment with different size brushes.

When your diya is dry, put it on display.

aarti—A type of worship with lamps, chants, and words to the gods.

annakut—A traditional Hindu service for which food is prepared for the gods in great quantity.

Ayodhya—Ancient city where Lord Rama was said to have reigned as king.

Bharata—Rama's stepbrother, who was supposed to become king when Rama was exiled.

Brahamanas—Ancient book of rules for rituals and explanations of why the rituals are important.

Dasaratha—Aging father of Rama, who was forced to send Rama into exile.

Deepavali—Another word for Diwali meaning "an array of lights."

dharma—Important Hindu term meaning "law," "duty," "justice," and "virtuousness."

dhoti—The traditional outfit of Indian men; it wraps around like a long skirt.

diyas—Clay lamps traditionally used as lights for Diwali.

dupatta—A narrow scarf that can be worn over the head or draped over the shoulder.

Dussehra—Holiday exactly twenty days before Diwali; the exact date that Rama killed the ancient demon Ravana.

guru—A Hindu teacher.

Kaikeyi—Rama's evil stepmother who forced him into exile.

kajal—Black eyeliner worn during Diwali to scare off evil spirits.

Kumkum—The substance that women use to create the red dot on their forehead.

Labh Pancham—The fifth day of the Hindu New Year, and often the day when businesses reopen after the holidays.

Mahabharata—One of the two major books of Hindu epic poems.

moksha—A Hindu term meaning "liberation."

moti choor ladoo—Among the most famous of all Diwali sweets.

murtis—Statues or images of the Hindu gods.

Nachiketa—Young boy who met Lord Yama, god of death, and was surprised by his gentleness.

Narakasur—Demon king slain by Lord Krishna.

nirvana—A perfect state of being full of inner peace; "the highest state of happiness."

nomads—People who spend much of their lives traveling from one place to another. Many people of ancient Asia, which is now India, were nomads.

pauva—A semi-cooked rice used to celebrate the harvest during Diwali.

Parvati—Goddess and wife of Lord Shiva, said to be responsible for the tradition of gambling during Diwali.

Prabhatiyas—Holy or uplifting songs generally sung only in the morning.

Pramukh Swami Maharaj—Considered the most important leader of Hinduism by many people.

prasad—An offering to the gods.

puja—Rituals of worship that honor the Hindu deities.

puja ghar—A place of worship.

Puranas—Ancient Hindu books containing myths and legends.

puri—A wheat flour dough used to make fried pita bread.

Ramayana—One of the two major books of Hindu poetry, containing the epic adventures of Rama and Sita.

rangoli—A powder used by children to make colorful designs on houses and sidewalks.

Ravana—The evil demon slain by Rama in the wilderness.

sakar—Little cubes of sugar.

Sanskrit—The classical language of India and Hinduism.

sari—A woman's traditional dress in India.

satsang—A gathering of people to worship.

Satyabhama—The wife of Lord Krishna who helped with the slaying of the evil demon Narakasur.

Subhadra—Sister of Lord Krishna, who first put the red dot called the tilak on Krishna's forehead.

Surpanaka—The evil sister of the demon Ravana.

thaal—A dish prepared for the gods.

tika—A type of tilak made of saffron and rice.

tilak—The red dot on a Hindu person's forehead.

uptan—A fragrant paste used in ritual bathing.

Vedas—Four books of sacred Hindu songs, rituals, and literature.

Yama—God of death; sometimes known as Yam.

CHAPTER NOTES

Chapter 1. The Story of Rama and Sita

1. Wendy O'Flaherty, *Hindu Mythology* (New York: Penguin Book Ltd., 1987), pp. 179–181.

2. "Hindu Gods and Goddesses: Lakshmi," *Indian Heritage*, n.d., <http://www.indian-heritage.org/gods/lakshmi.htm> (August 13, 2006).

3. W. J. Wilkins, *Hindu Mythology* (New York: Asian Book Corporation of America, 1987), p. 190, quoting Griffith's Ramayana, iv. 334.

4. Ibid., pp. 191–193.

5. Ibid., p. 195.

6. Wilkins, p. 196.

7. Ibid.

8. Ibid.

9. Elizabeth Breuilly, Joanne O'Brien, and Martin Palmer, *Festivals of the World: The Illustrated Guide to Celebrations, Customs, Events and Holidays* (New York: Checkmark Books, 2002), pp. 84–85.

Chapter 2. History of Diwali

1. "Frequently Asked Questions: Where and when did Hinduism begin?" *Seek and You Shall Find*, n.d.,

<http://www.hindudevotion.com/faq.html>
(November 9, 2006).

2. Steven Knapp, "About the Name Hindu," *Proof of Vedic Culture's Global Existence*, n.d., <http://www.stephen-knapp.com/about_the_name_Hindu.htm> (April 3, 2006).

3. Ibid.

4. Elizabeth Breuilly, Joanne O'Brien, and Martin Palmer, *Festivals of the World: The Illustrated Guide to Celebrations, Customs, Events and Holidays* (New York: Checkmark Books, 2002), p. 83.

5. Gavin Flood, *An Introduction to Hinduism* (New York: Cambridge University Press, 1996), pp. 105–107.

6. Knapp.

7. Pujya, Swamiji, "Religion and Culture in the New Millennium," *Articles from Drops of Nectar*, n.d., <http://www.ihrf.com/publi/drops/dropsreligion.htm> (April 4, 2006).

8. Ed Viswanathan, *Am I Hindu?* (San Francisco: Halo Books, 1992), p. 1.

9. Flood, p. 12.

10. "Festivals and Fairs of Maharashtra," *Maharashtra*, n.d., <http://www.t2maharashtra.com/events2.php> (August 14, 2006).

11. "Dhanteras," *I Love India*, n.d., <http://festivals.iloveindia.com/diwali/dhanteras.html> (April 4, 2006).

12. "Choti-Diwali," *I Love India*, n.d., <http://festivals.iloveindia.com/diwali/choti-diwali.html> (April 4, 2006).

13. "Choti Diwali," *Diwali, Festival of Lights*, n.d., <http://www.diwalifestival.org/choti-diwali.html> (April 4, 2006).

14. "Diwali—The Origin," *Diwali*, n.d., <http://www.the holidayspot.com/diwali/origin.htm> (April 4, 2006).

15. Elizabeth Breuilly, Joanne O'Brien, and Martin Palmer, p. 87.

16. Wilkins, pp. 197–199.

17. "Padwa & Govardhan Puja," *Diwali, Festival of Lights*, n.d., <http://www.diwalifestival.org/padwa-govardhan-puja.html> (April 4, 2006).

18. "Significance of Diwali," *Mataya World—Diwali*, n.d., <http://www.matiyapatidar.com/diwali_fest.htm> (April 4, 2006).

19. Malini Bisen, "Diwali," *Barwarchi Festivals*, n.d., <www.bawarchi.com/festivals/diwali1.html> (April 4, 2006).

20. Ibid.

21. "The Third Day of Diwali," *Festivals of India*, n.d., <http://www.festivalsofindia.in/diwali/Third.asp> (August 14, 2006).

◆ Chapter 3. The Cultural Significance of Diwali

1. "Making Diwali Rangoli," *Diwali, The Festival of Lights*, n.d., <http://www.diwalifestival.org/making-diwali-rangoli.html> (August 14, 2006).

2. Pramesh Ratnakar, *Hinduism* (New York: Heian International Publishers, 1999), p. 75.

3. Ibid., p. 76.

4. Personal interview with Vaishali Patel, March 22, 2006.

5. Personal interview with Pramesh Ratnakar, March 22, 2006.

6. Ibid.

7. Gavin Flood, *An Introduction to Hinduism* (New York: Cambridge University Press, 1996), p. 209.

8. Chantal Boulenger, "Nivi Saris," *Saris: An Illustrated Guide to the Indian Art of Draping*, n.d., <http://www.devi.net/shakti/sari/nivi.html> (August 12, 2006).

9. Ibid., "Kaccha Saris," n.d., <http://www.devi.net/shakti/sari/kaccha.html> (August 12, 2006).

10. Pramesh Ratnakar, *Hinduism* (New Delhi, India: Roli and Janssen BV, 2004), p. 70.

11. "Diwali in Delhi," *Diwali, the Festival of Lights*, n.d., <http://www.diwalifestival.org/diwali-in-delhi.html> (August 14, 2006).

12. Personal interview with Parimal Parikh, March 13, 2006.

13. Personal interview with Vaishali Patel, March 22, 2006.

Chapter 4. Who Celebrates Diwali and Diwali Influences

1. Matt Rosenberg, "India," *The CIA Fact Book*, n.d., <http://geography.about.com/library/cia/blcindia.htm> (April 4, 2006).

2. "Choti Diwali / Narak Chaturdasi," *Diwali, Festival of Lights*, n.d., <http://www.diwalifestival.org/choti-diwali.html> (August 14, 2006).

3. Malini Bisen, "Diwali," *Bawarchi Festivals*, n.d., <www.bawarchi.com/festivals/diwali1.html> (April 4, 2006).

4. "Diwali in North India," *Diwali, The Festival of Lights*, n.d., <http://www.diwalifestival.org/diwali-in-north-india.html> (August 14, 2006).

5. Bisen.

6. Manmohan Melville, "At Divali—Life Is a Divine Gamble," *Gateway for India*, n.d., <http://www.gatewayforindia.com/culture/divali.htm> (April 4, 2006).

7. "Diwali as Harvest Festival," *Diwali, The Festival of Lights*, n.d., <http://www.diwalifestival.org/diwali-as-harvest-festival.html> (August 14, 2006).

8. "India," *World Fact Book of the Central Intelligence Agency*, August 8, 2006, <http://www.cia.gov/cia/publications/factbook/geos/in.html> (August 14, 2006).

9. "Census of India: 2001," *Office of the Registrar General, India, March 1, 2001*, n.d., <http://www.censusindia.net/profiles/bih.html> (August 14, 2006).

10. "Diwali in Bihar," *Diwali, The Festival of Lights*, n.d., <http://www.diwalifestival.org/diwali-in-bihar.html> (August 14, 2006).

11. "Diwali in Delhi," *Diwali, The Festival of Lights*, n.d., <http://www.diwalifestival.org/diwali-in-delhi.html> (August 14, 2006).

12. "Diwali in Gujarat," *Diwali, The Festival of Lights*, n.d., <http://www.diwalifestival.org/diwali-in-gujarat.html> (August 14, 2006).

13. "Sukhsuptika." *India9: The Information Source for India*, n.d., <http://www.india9.com/i9show/Sukhsuptika-55397.htm> (April 4, 2006).

14. Bisen.

15. "Diwali in Maharashtra," *Diwali, The Festival of Lights*, n.d., <http://www.diwalifestival.org/diwali-in-maharashtra.html> (August 14, 2006).

16. "Why is Diwali Important to Sikhs?" *Sikh Study Circle*, n.d., <http://www.sikhstudy.com/diwali_for_sikhs.html> (August 14, 2006).

17. Gavin Flood, *An Introduction to Hinduism* (New York: Cambridge University Press, 1996), p. 209.

18. "Diwali in Orissa," *Diwali, The Festival of Lights*, n.d., <http://www.diwalifestival.org/diwali-in-orissa.html> (August 14, 2006).

19. "Diwali in West Bengal," *Diwali, The Festival of Lights*, n.d., <http://www.diwalifestival.org/diwali-in-west-bengal.htm> (August 14, 2006).

20. Carol Stultsky, "Cities of Burning, Towns of Teaching," *Namaste: A Journey Through Spiritual India*, March 18, 2006, <http://www.coveringreligion.org/2006/03/18/varanasi_1.html> (October 3, 2006).

21. "Himachal Pradesh: Fairs and Festivals," *WebIndia123*, n.d., <http://www.webindia123.com/Himachal/festivals/festivals3.htm> (August 14, 2006).

◆ **Chapter 5. Holiday Symbols**

1. Malini Bisen, "Diwali," *Bawarchi Festivals*, n.d., <www.bawarchi.com/festivals/diwali2.html> (April 4, 2006).

2. Ibid.

3. "Dussehra and Diwali," *Maharashtra Tourism*, n.d., <http://www.maharashtratourism.gov.in/mtdc/Default.aspx?strpage=festivals_diwali.html> (August 14, 2006).

4. "Hindu Gods and Goddesses," *Sanatan Society*, n.d., <http://www.sanatansociety.org/hindu_gods_and_goddesses.htm> (August 14, 2006).

5. "Hinduism: Bindis: What You Need to Know," *About.com*, n.d., <http://hinduism.about.com/library/weekly/aa072002a.htm> (September 13, 2006).

6. Stephen Knapp, "Lakshmi, the Goddess of Fortune," n.d., <http://www.stephen-knapp.com/lakshmi_goddess_of_fortune.htm> (14 Aug 2006).

7. Personal interview with Vaishali Patel, March 22, 2006.

8. Personal interview with Parimal Parikh, March 12, 2006.

9. Gavin Flood, *An Introduction to Hinduism* (New York: Cambridge University Press, 1996), p. 212.

◆ Chapter 6. Diwali Celebrations Around the World

1. "Stories and Photos about Life in Thailand: 'Deeparaya' in Malaysia," *Paknam Web Network*, November 1, 2005, <http://www.thai-blogs.com/index.php?p=843&more=1&c=1&tb=1&pb=1> (September 13, 2006).

2. "PM's Call to Strengthen Bonds on Diwali," *The Travel Times*, n.d., <http://www.indiatraveltimes.com/malaysia/news.html#malay> (April 4, 2006).

3. "Diwali in Nepal," *Diwali, The Festival of Lights*, n.d., <http://www.diwalifestival.org/diwali-in-nepal.html> (August 14, 2006).

4. Ibid.

5. "Ram Katha by Morari Bapu-to be Telecasted Live on Aastha TV," *AASTHA Television Channel*, May 10, 2002, <http://www.aasthatv.com/pressdetails.htm> (April 4, 2006).

6. "Diwali Celebrations Around the World," *TheHolidaySpot*, n.d., <http://www.theholidayspot.com/diwali/around_the_world.htm> (August 12, 2006).

7. "Create Diwali Gift Hampers for Friends and Family," *Bombshell Designs*, n.d., <http://www.bombshellbrands.com/diwali-gift-hampers.html> (August 11, 2006).

8. "South African President Greets Indian Diaspora on Diwali," *Indo-Asian News Service*, November 14, 2001, <http://www.rediff.com/us/2001/nov/14sa.htm> (April 4, 2006).

9. "Sabdavali Glossary," *Himalayan Academy Hindu Basics*, n.d., <http://www.worldebooklibrary.com/eBooks/HimalayanAcademy/SacredHinduLiteratur e/lg/lg_glossary.html> (August 12, 2006).

10. Kurma Dasa, "Classic Indian Sweets," *Cooking with Kurma*, July 25, 2006, <http://www.kurma.net/essays/e16.html> (August 11, 2006).

11. "Diwali," *Traveljournals.net*, November 1, 2005, <http://www.traveljournals.net/stories/10090.html> (April 4, 2006).

12. "Diwali Celebrations Around the World."

13. Mackintosh, Bryan, "Guyana Diwali Motorcade 2005," November 2005, <http://www.motorsports guyana.com/diwali05.htm > (April 4, 2006).

14. "Diwali Celebrations Around the World."

15. "Holy See's Message to Hindus on Feast of Diwali," *Catholic Insight*, December 1, 2003, vol. 11, p. 10:23.

16. "Hindu Americans: Rising Numbers—Shining Contributions," *Introduction to Hinduism*, n.d., <http://www.hinduamericanfoundation.org/hintro _rising_numbers.htm> (August 13, 2006).

17. Personal interview with Vaishali Patel, March 22, 2006.

18. "1st Diwali at Gracie Mansion," *DesiTalk*, November 26, 2004, <http://www.desitalk.com/dit/2004/11/26/index.html> (October 29, 2006).

19. "Diwali and New Year's Celebrations 2003," *BAPS Swaminarayan Society*, October 2003, <http://www.baps.org/news/usa/2003/10/diwaliannakut /index.htm> (August 13, 2006).

20. "Diwali and Annakut Utsav 2004: USA. and Canada," *BAPS Swaminarayan Society*, n.d., <http://www.swaminarayan.org/news/usa/2004/11/diwaliannakut/overview.htm> (August 13, 2006).

21. Personal interview with Anthony Fargo, March 13, 2006.

22. "Diwali and New Year's Celebrations 2003—USA and Canada," *BAPS Swaminarayan Society*, n.d., <http://www.swaminarayan.org/news/usa/2003/10/diwaliannakut/index.htm> (August 13, 2006).

23. Personal interview with Vaishali Patel, March 22, 2006.

24. Pramesh Ratnakar, *Hinduism*, (New York: Heian International Publishers, 1999), p. 221.

FURTHER READING

Books

Ganeri, Anita. *Hindu Festivals Throughout the Year.* Mankato, Minn.: Smart Apple Media, 2003.

George, Charles. *What Makes Me a Hindu?* San Diego, Calif.: KidHaven Press, 2004.

Gibson, Lynne. *Hinduism.* Austin, Tex.: Raintree Steck-Vaughn Publishers, 2003.

Jani, Mahendra, and Vandana Jani. *What You Will See Inside a Hindu Temple.* Woodstock, Vt.: SkyLight Paths Pub., 2005.

Mattern, Joanne. *India.* Mankato, Minn.: Bridgestone Books, 2003.

Weitzman, David. *Rama and Sita: A Tale of Ancient Java.* Boston, Mass.: D. R. Godine, 2002.

INTERNET ADDRESSES

Hindu Gods and Goddesses
<http://www.sanatansociety.org/hindu_gods_and_goddesses.htm>
Click on the illustrations to find out more about the Hindu gods and goddesses.

Indian Festivals: Diwali
<http://www.sscnet.ucla.edu/southasia/Culture/Festivals/Diwali.html>
Learn more about Diwali at this Web site.

INDEX

A

aarti, 47, 60, 86
annakut, 51–52, 86, 105
Ayodhya, 7, 12, 13, 19,
    31, 74

B

Bhai Duj, 33–34
Bihar, 61–62
Brahamanas, 22–23

C

Chopada Puja, 29–31
Choti Diwali, 27–29, 45

D

Delhi, 62–64
Dhantrayodashi, 25–27,
    28
dharma, 22, 81
dhoti, 49–50
diyas, 42–44, 50, 55, 73,
    74, 90, 95, 98
dupatta, 49
Dussehra, 35, 62–63

G

Govardhan Puja, 33
Great Britain, 96
Gujarat, 44, 49, 64, 83
Guyana, 90, 96–98

H

Himachal Pradesh, 71

K

Kaikeyi, 7–8
Kashmir, 65
Kumkum, 58, 76

L

Labh Pancham, 64
Lakshmi, 6, 7, 12,
    29–31, 40, 42–44, 45,
    46, 54, 60, 62, 64,
    65, 67, 69, 71, 77,
    79–83, 92, 96

M

Mahabharata, 19
Maharashtra, 65–66
Malaysia, 90–91

Mauritius, 93–94

moksha, 22, 81

murtis, 50–51

N

Nachiketa, 36

Narakasur, 28, 33, 58, 76

Nepal, 56, 61, 91–93

nirvana, 22, 34

O

Orissa, 68–69

P

Padwa, 31–33

Parvati, 60

Pramukh Swami Maharaj, 60

prasad, 51, 69

Punjab, 55, 67–68

Puranas, 4, 19, 35

R

Rama, 5–13, 14, 19, 29, 31, 33, 35, 52, 62, 64, 74, 77, 87, 93

Ramayana, 6–7, 10, 13, 19, 23, 35, 77

rangoli, 40–42, 62, 64, 68

Ravana, 10–12, 35, 62, 63, 74, 87

S

Sanskrit, 7, 19, 25, 81, 84

sari, 46–49

Satyabhama, 28,

Shiva, 60, 87, 91

Sita, 5–12, 19, 29, 35, 52, 64, 74, 77, 95

South Africa, 94–96

Subhadra, 33–34

Surpanaka, 8–10

T

tilak, 34, 67, 76–79

U

Uttar Pradesh, 69–71

V

Vedas, 18–19, 22

Vishnu, 6, 12, 14, 15, 33, 36, 46, 77, 81, 83

W

West Bengal, 69

Y

Yama, 27, 36, 44, 74–75, 91

DATE DUE